1

NAKED TRUTHS ABOUT
GETTING PRODUCT REVIEWS
on Amazon.com

7 Insider tips to boost Sales

Copyright © 2016 and 2017 by Gisela Hausmann
Published by Educ-Easy Books
www.giselahausmann.com

* * *

ISBN 978-0-9968972-0-4

Fully updated and revised April 8, 2017

* * *

Editor:
Divya Lavanya

* * *

***

CONTENT:

The greatness of reviews 10

This book was written for Amazon vendors worldwide 11

That's Me 12

Past Problems 14

Reviews and the FTC 16

On October 3, 2016 Amazon notably changed its Community Guidelines 18

What not to say when asking for reviews 20

Why Reviews Matter – Let's look at the details 26

The real problem with the absence of reviews 28

Search Engine Rankings – Reviews help in getting your products' reviews seen on Google 31

Products need different types of reviews 36

7 TYPES OF REVIEWS

The "I just want to say 'I love this'" review 37

The Typical Customer Review 38

The Technical Review 38

The Venting Review 38

The Funny Review   40

The Short-Story Review   41

The Top Reviewer or Hall of Fame Reviewer's Review   41

7 TIPS HOW TO BOOST SALES

1) Learn from reviews   43

What to do if your product gets a negative review   47

Trolls   49

Why do customers trust reviewers they don't even know?   52

How to find Reviewers

TIP 2) How to find reviewers who write technical reviews   53

TIP 3) How to find reviewers who write funny reviews?   55

TIP 4) How to find reviewers who write "I just want to say 'I love this'" reviews   56

TIP 5) How to find reviewers who write typical customer reviews?   58

TIP 6) Update your Customer Service Information and make reading reviews part of your Customer Service agents' job description   59

TIP 7) How to find all kinds of reviewers - The best tip of all   63

How to encourage customers to review?   66

Finally – Where should you start? 70

TO-DO LISTS **71**

Gisela Hausmann's business philosophy about "naked (meaning no-fluff) books" 74

About the Author 77

Other books 78

The greatness of reviews

When you attempt to find out how you can improve sales on the Amazon platform, you'll learn about Amazon Pay Per Click campaigns (PPC), brand-building, brand management, building a targeted launch, effective keyword bid optimization, growth strategy, getting traffic via social media ads, getting more organic reach, mobile media buying, and hundreds of other strategies and concepts.

While all of this is/may be important, absolutely nothing beats the effect of thousands and thousands of reviews. Every consumer knows that they don't review every product they use. Hence, it is clear that if a product has 10,000 verified reviews, at least 100,000 people bought this product.

As of today, Amazon's Fire TV Stick with Alexa Voice Remote features 188,693 customer reviews and 1000+ answered questions.

To test the power of reviews, tell a technology challenged elderly person, "Guess what? Amazon's Fire Stick has more than 188,000 reviews" and they are probably going to reply, "Really? What does this Fire Stick do?"

Tell the same thing to a seven year old and they are probably going to reply, "Can I get one?"

Such is the power of reviews, which is why you should do everything to help your product acquire as many reviews as possible. All other strategies will work better if your product has lots of reviews.

This book was written for Amazon vendors worldwide

There are a lot of similarities between the Amazon river and jungle and the Amazon store. This is an aerial photograph of the Amazon river winding through the jungle by the same name.

Maybe, you sometimes feel like explorer Francisco de Orellana might have felt when he set off to explore the South American interior in search of El Dorado, the "city of gold."

This book will show you ways to help charting your course. Since buyers find products with many reviews very attractive, web-savvy vendors and manufacturers actively encourage customers to leave reviews.

That's Me

Gisela Hausmann

About *Public*
author, mail evangelist, Amazon review expert

Currently (since Amazon changed its Community Guidelines) NOT accepting books and/or free products. If you need to find out how to find reviewers please read my books. Thank you! Author of "Naked Truths About Getting Book Reviews" and "Naked Truths About Getting Product Reviews"

Reviewer ranking
#2,756

Insights

6	1.2k	577	0	0
followers *Private*	helpful votes *Public*	reviews *Public*	hearts *Public*	idea lists *Public*

Hello, I am Gisela Hausmann. My best reviewer ranking was #2,756 out of 65+ million reviewers. I began reviewing at Amazon in 2012. In 2014, I reached Amazon Top Reviewer ranking, consistently being ranked in Amazon's Top-10,000.

Becoming an Amazon Top Reviewer is not easy. Reviewers are ranked not only by the number of reviews they write, but also by the numbers of "likes" their reviews garner.

Potential buyers are picky. They don't like every review. They **want to know**

- technical specifications,
- potential product flaws,
- how user friendly the product is,
- what makes the product outstanding,

and, most importantly

- how will they feel if they buy a certain product? Will it make their life better, more pleasurable, easier... and – Why?

Having graduated with a master's degree in Film and Mass Media from the University of Vienna, I find this new way of information exchange, which can be combined with effective marketing, fascinating. To acquire the information listed in this book, I have studied thousands of reviews and checked their effects by looking at thousands of book and product sales ranks.

My work as an Amazon ecommerce expert has been featured on *Bloomberg* (podcast) and on *NBC News* (blog); my work as an email evangelist was featured in the *SUCCESS* magazine and in *Entrepreneur*. I am also a frequent guest, speaking about communications topics, on WYFF-4, my local NBC TV-station.

Past Problems

While in the past Amazon used to introduce gradual, small changes to its Community Guidelines, unexpectedly, on October 3, 2016, they made a *huge* change.

Since that day, manufacturers and vendors may not request reviews the way they used to do, for years. Now, offering free or discounted products *in exchange* for a product review is a violation of Amazon's Community Guidelines.

This development is significant because offering free sample products in exchange for honest and unbiased reviews was a great way to get *starter reviews* for a product launch on Amazon.

Sadly, a few years ago, some ecommerce vendors cheated and "purchased" reviews. After Amazon dealt with this issue, some vendors resorted to offering free products instead of paying for reviews. Others encouraged people who wanted to receive free merchandise to join clubs that served as platforms to bring interested parties together. Logically, these options did not necessarily lead to getting best reviews from the most qualified reviewers. This "incentivized" process was about amassing reviews instead of getting quality starter reviews.

Amazon also made it a requirement that reviewers must spend at least $50.00 per year on Amazon before they can post a review. Simply being a registered customer who may have bought only one ebook for $0.99 is not good enough anymore. This new requirement seemed to suggest that fake reviewers tried to open multiple accounts to place reviews. Obviously, with the new rule in place, opening ten (fake) accounts would cost $500.00, which should discourage fake reviewers to go that route.

Also, over the last two years, I personally got pursued relentlessly by Chinese manufacturers and vendors who wanted me to review their products. These organizations did not do what I recommended in the first edition of my book; they did not look for "perfect (best match) Amazon top reviewers." They probably contacted every reviewer whose email address they could find.

In my case, at least twice per month, I received requests to review dog products which proved that these review seekers could not possibly have looked up my reviewer profile. The fact that I never reviewed dog products made it quite obvious that I don't have a dog. Hence, these vendors were spamming me.

In short, though I personally have no knowledge about any abuse of Amazon's review system, I have guesses as to how some tried to do just that.

There are three lessons to be learned:

1. Getting product reviews will really help the sales of your product; otherwise, there would not be so many vendors who try to cheat.

2. It is in the nature of the Internet-beast that cheaters will try to exploit opportunities. Do not follow their lead. Since every reviewer has to log in to post a review, Amazon's algorithms can identify "unusual activities;" over the last few years, Amazon has stripped thousands of reviewers of their review privileges and also deleted these reviewers' reviews.

3. Shooting spray, meaning contacting everybody whose email address you can find including people who probably don't have use for your product will not lead to great results but annoy reviewers.
    It might also prompt Amazon to impose more restrictions.

Reviews and the FTC

The fact that reviews are so important for the sales of products and purchases led to the "fake review scandal" of the last few years. This scandal evolved at many well-known ecommerce sites (Amazon, Yelp, Tripadvisor, and other sites).

The problem was that an unknown number of merchants, service providers, and authors purchased fake product reviews. The reviewers-for-hire never used the products or read the books, and they never slept in the hotels they reviewed. Some of these reviews sold for as little as $5.00.

Posting fake reviews is illegal in most countries. In the United States, posting a fake review (positive or negative) breaks the Federal Trade Commission's truth-in-advertising laws. Please find more information about this topic at the FTC's website.

https://www.ftc.gov/tips-advice/business-center/advertising-and-marketing/online-advertising-and-marketing

Obviously, being able to find out what other consumers thought about a particular product or service is only helpful if the reviews are honest.

To combat this problem, in 2011, Cornell University developed an algorithm to detect fake reviews. Ecommerce websites (including Amazon) refined this algorithm for their specific needs and also developed filters to block fake reviews. Additionally, all ecommerce sites posted strict guidelines for the creation of reviews; they also reserve themselves the right to delete any review which does not meet these guidelines.

To take matters even further, on December 12, 2015 Amazon filed a lawsuit against 1,114 people who allegedly offered to write such reviews, at a price of five dollars a review.

Summing it up – These days, ecommerce sites will go through great lengths to ensure the integrity of their review systems. It is in the interest of all vendors to support these efforts.

On October 3, 2016 Amazon notably changed its Community Guidelines

Obviously, the burden to filter out fake reviews lies with ecommerce sites. While the FTC is not going to hunt down individual fake reviewers, they require that ecommerce stores create rules that make it impossible or nearly impossible for fake reviewers to post.

On October 3, 2016 Amazon took more steps to ensure just that.

The three most significant changes for vendors are:

1. To post customer reviews or customer answers, or post on forums, customers must have spent at least $50 on Amazon.com using a valid credit or debit card. The reason for this change seems to be that some "fake reviewers" opened multiple accounts to do their "dirty deeds."

2. Vendors cannot request reviews any longer like they used to be able to do. Offering or requesting compensation, in form of free or discounted products, in exchange for writing a review is no longer an option.

3. When manufacturers and/or vendors post an answer to a question asked through the Q/A feature on Amazon they have to clearly disclose their connection and with it their interests. (e.g., "I am the manufacturer or vendor of this product.").

It is immensely important that you study these review guidelines and re-read them every month! Nobody knows when Amazon decides to make changes. During the last two years, Amazon changed its community guidelines six times without warning.

Always re-read the guidelines before you launch a promotion that is geared at receiving many reviews.

http://www.amazon.com/gp/community-help/customer-reviews-guidelines

What not to say when asking for reviews:

Whether Amazon allows it or not, every day, thousands of product vendors ask for reviews. Though I deleted my email address on Amazon's site in November 2016, I still get up to ten review requests every day.

How do vendors get my email address?

A few organizations sell or give away as a bonus an outdated list of Amazon top reviewers.

How can you be sure that these lists outdated?

Amazon disconnected the email addresses of their top reviewers in March 2017. Since then, Amazon also stripped hundreds of top reviewers of their review privileges. Consequently, hundreds of new reviewers moved up the ranks. These new top reviewers' email addresses were never listed on Amazon.

Vendors who disregard these widely known facts and request reviews from top reviewers need to try hard. Here are a few examples *what not to write,* for your amusement:

***

"... I understand you are a reliable, experienced reviewer..."

> *[Really? Who told you that?...]*

***

"... Dear Mary,
I found a review on Amazon that you wrote for (product) ..."

> *[Who is Mary?]*

"... As a top reviewer, you always provide honest and helpful reviews that help shoppers to have a better shopping experience and encourage us to improve our products.
We recently launched a few new products (category: dog products), we need hear your voice..."

> [Dear friend,
> You don't need to hear my voice, you need to learn doing better research.
> Simply scanning over my reviews would reveal that I never reviewed a single dog product.
> It probably doesn't take Sherlock Holmes to figure out that I don't have a dog.]

***

"... Our company needs US reviews. May I know if you interested? We sell lights, indoor and outdoor. If you are interested, please kindly reply with your profile, thank you..."

> [Ahh... You need US reviews but want me to 'apply for the unpaid job' by sending you my reviewer profile? That suggests that you may have purchased a list of reviewers' email addresses. Try to get your money back and good luck.]

***

"... As a valued customer of (company), we would like to invite you to take part in future new product introductions. When we launch a new product, we'd reach out to you and offer..."

> [Utter nonsense!! I never purchased a single product from your company..
> It appears you stringing together big words and email them to random people.
> Are you planning a career in politics?]

"... You've been handpicked as a highly qualified reviewer..."

> [Hand-picked? This wording sounds as if I had been selected for a dangerous clandestine operation...
> Thx, but no thanks...]

***

"... I would really value your opinion! ..."

> [Dear friend,
> The word 'really' is kind of amusing. I spent enough time online to know that most vendors value most good reviews and that they vent about bad reviews.]

***

"... I am impressed with how well you've done with your thoughtful product reviews..."

> [Dear friend,
> May I ask what you mean by "how well you've done with your thoughtful product reviews?"
> Reviewing books and products is a hobby, not a career.]

***

"... Dear Top Reviewer,
Congratulations! You have been pre-selected to join ... xyz... Club. Registration is by invitation only.
Joining is completely FREE!
You will get a chance to test brand-new products, completely FREE. This offer is limited to 50 people, so please register a.s.a.p. to avoid disappointment..."

> [Dear friend,
> I am curious. Did you ever have to disappoint somebody?]

"... I just started to sell a brand new product, and I need your help with testing and reviewing it.
Since you are one Amazon's top reviewers your review is important to me and to our customers..."

> *[Is this your best pitch — describing what's important to YOU?]*

***

"Any updates?
Just following up on the email I sent a week ago."
THX,
(name)

> *[No. No updates!*
>
> *Fun Fact: On average, American professionals receive approximately 120 emails and send about 40 emails per day. Not every sender makes the cut, for obvious reasons.]*

***

"... One of my problems is that I may be too impatient and at the same time too lazy. Can you recommend a way how to get reviews via review marketing services..."

> *[Dear friend,*
> *I truly value your honesty.*
> *Hence, here is my honest advice:*
> *Stop being lazy and impatient. In all of history, not one single person succeeded by being lazy or impatient. And, no, throwing money at the problem won't work. Today consumers want to hear customers' authentic voices.]*

***

"... Dear Top Reviewer,
We Need 12 US Top Reviewers for a (product) right now,
Full Refund by Paypal or Amazon gift card..."

[There is nothing like a Take-the-Bull-by-the-Horns approach in the spirit of 'Take it or leave it!' ...
I guess you read "The Art of the Deal" by Donald Trump.
There is only one major problem with your proposal — your offer is not a deal!

Your offer is in violation of Amazon's community guidelines, hence you have to be insane to think that I would accept it.
Becoming a top reviewer takes a few years. Do you really think I risk losing my reviewer privileges and five years of work for the chance to review your $20.00 product?]

***

"... I wanted to get in touch with you after coming across your sincere and insightful reviews on Amazon..."

[How kind of you!
You aren't just saying that, right? You really read some of my reviews?]

***

"... Since Amazon's new policy prohibits to exchange reviews, I was wondering if we could work together in a different way. We are looking for reviewers; we pay $15-30 per review via Paypal..."

[Huh?
Amazon's guidelines forbid authors and sellers to offer any kind of compensation in exchange for a review.
Here is some advice: It's one thing to pretend to be stupid, it's a completely different thing to say, "I know that my

request is a violation of the rules but let's call it something 'different'," and spell it out — in black on white.]

***

"...Hi Gisela Hausmann:
I am [...name...]. I have found your reviwer profile info from amazon. you are alway been doing notary review for every product that is why you are very important for us ,Your reviwe will makes a significant difference to us as a small business..."

> *[Dear friend,*
> *A) You are lying. I deleted my email address on Amazon's reviewer list, almost two years ago.*
> *B) Certainly, being a small business owner isn't easy. However, hiring a translator on Fiverr costs only five dollars.*
>
> *Since, apparently, you are not willing to invest even such a small amount of money plus you are lying about where you got my email address, I don't care to test your product. Quite obviously, you are cutting corners wherever you can.]*

***

There are also product vendors who offer to ship products for free, no strings attached, in the hope that reviewers will review them. Other product vendors inform reviewers of steeply discounted products. Both of these efforts may work.

However, it is highly unlikely that a reputable top reviewer will accept any kind of "pay-for-review"-offer. Amazon strips reviewers who they catch engaging in such efforts of their reviewer privileges, mercilessly.

Why Reviews Matter – Let's look at the details

Amazon pioneered customers reviews only 21 years ago; today, people over the age forty can't even remember how they made purchasing decisions when they had to rely on word of mouth and various consumer report magazines.

Even people, who, by principle, do not shop at Amazon (e.g. because they want to support their local neighborhood store), read reviews at Amazon's website; especially if they intend to buy a high-ticket item. Today's customers want to make smart buying decisions; they also check reviews because it is so easy.

Motivated by the same concept, people who buy products at other stores leave reviews at Amazon, either to proclaim how fabulous the product is or to vent about a purchase which turned out to be not-as-satisfying as they thought it would be.

There is more! Savvy second-hand shoppers, who scan craigslist or brick-and-mortar second-hand stores for valuable purchases, consult product reviews, too. These customers want to know what the original price of the item was and what other buyers are saying. There is always the possibility that the original buyer is trying to get rid of an item because it did not live up to his expectations.

Needless to say, if these extremely savvy shoppers find an excellent deal, they will also be the first ones to spread the word about a great product they acquired, thereby marketing it.

Amazon's platform supports our 21st century lifestyle of

- announcing our impressions and opinions openly, on the Internet,
- connecting with strangers to talk about things that are important to us or to them, and
- feeling solidarity with potential consumers, who we will never meet, but who we can help by sharing our findings.

Brick-and-mortar stores are following the trend. American retailer Home Depot is using shelf hang tracks to tell potential customers how they can access product reviews at their website.

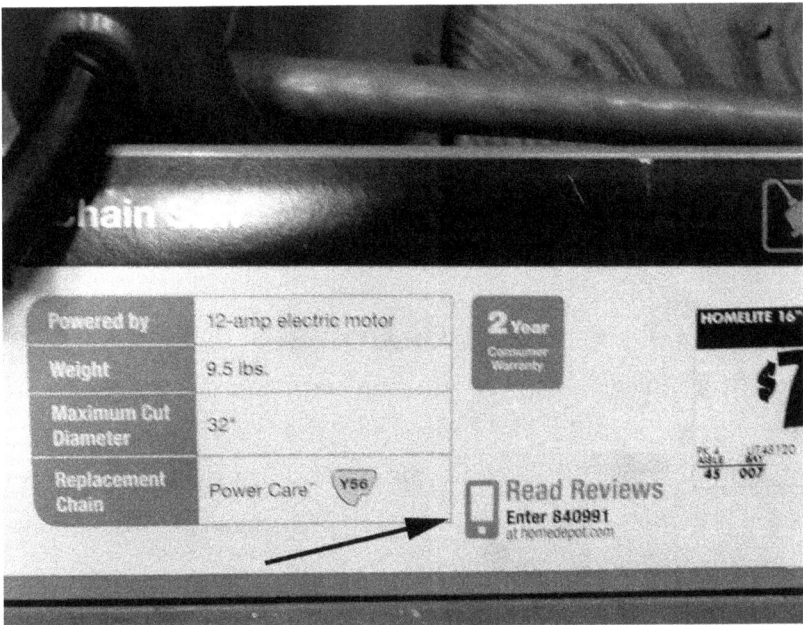

The real problem with the absence of reviews

While obviously the number of reviews is related to the quality of products and the demand for these products, the absence of reviews does not mean that a certain product isn't good or needed.

If a product has less than a dozen reviews, it means that the product did not have a great launch.

Here is an example which made me sad on a personal level.

As an Austrian immigrant who is living in the United States for almost three decades, I still miss some of the traditional holiday foods from my home country. Among these gourmet foods are Vanillekipferl, a type of traditional Austrian Christmas cookies which are extremely popular throughout central Europe. To bake the delicate crescent-shaped cookies requires a lot of work. Since I don't cook too often and hardly ever bake, I prefer to buy them.

In the summer of 2014, I spotted Wicklein Nuernberger Vanilla Crescent (Vanillekipferl) at Amazon.com and I purchased them immediately. Neither the price nor the fact that it was July mattered; for me, Christmas came early that year. I also reviewed these Christmas cookies and awarded them with 4 stars. Sadly, to this day my review is the only one.

The product is "currently unavailable;" it is no longer being distributed by any US company. I found out about this tragic situation when I intended to buy these cookies again, for my Christmas party.

It needs to be noted that Gottfried Wicklein GmbH & Co. KG, the German manufacturer of these cookies, has a stellar reputation.

Founded in 1615, the company is over 400 years old. Unquestionably, Wicklein produces fantastic baked goods.

Since the quality of the product is established, the following question arises: Would this product still be on the U.S. market if it was supported by many more reviews?

I believe so.

Currently, Amazon.com sells only one brand of Vanillekipferl by a different manufacturer. So far, only one person reviewed these other cookies and awarded them with only 2 stars. The review states explicitly that the cookies aren't delicate as they ought to be. So, I did not buy them.

Disappointed that I could not buy one of the products, which for me is intrinsically connected with Christmas celebrations, I kept on meandering through Amazon's vast store and ended up purchasing three Star Wars Adult Jedi Fleece Hooded Bath Robes, as Christmas gifts for my family. This bathrobe featured 138 reviews with an average rating of 4.4 out of 5 stars.

This little story describes the main issue for Amazon vendors: Vendors can promote their products as much as they want; once customers check out a product, on Amazon's website or in other stores, reviews have a major impact on the customers' decision to buy. Obviously, today customers can check online product reviews on their smartphones even while visiting brick and mortar stores. Millennials are especially known to do this as they have grown up with reading online reviews as well as using smartphones.

If a product does not have a lot of reviews, inevitably, potential buyers' eyes wander to other products, either in a store or on Amazon's website. Amazon goes through great efforts to present other products which buyers appreciated, bought, and reviewed. Meandering potential buyers may end up buying a competitor's product or a completely different product, just like I did.

Obviously, it is in Amazon's interest to make this browsing through different categories as easy as possible. Therefore vendors need to do everything they can to convince potential buyers that they need to buy their product *right then,* when they first look at its product page. The presence of many reviews helps with this decision.

Potential buyers want to know others' opinions.

Search Engine Rankings – Reviews help in getting your products' reviews seen on Google

It is well known that if people want to learn more about other people, they search on Facebook; if they want to check out products, they search on Google.

Therefore, I recommend that business owners and independent contractors, whose products are also for sale on Amazon, should encourage their customers to review their products on Amazon.

This will result in additional benefits; and they are free of cost.

Amazon's website ranks extremely high on all search engines, consistently. Even though my beloved Vanillekipferl are no longer available at Amazon.com, a search on Google will show these cookies on their Amazon page in the first position on Google. Notice also that the preview says "Read honest and unbiased product... (reviews)..."

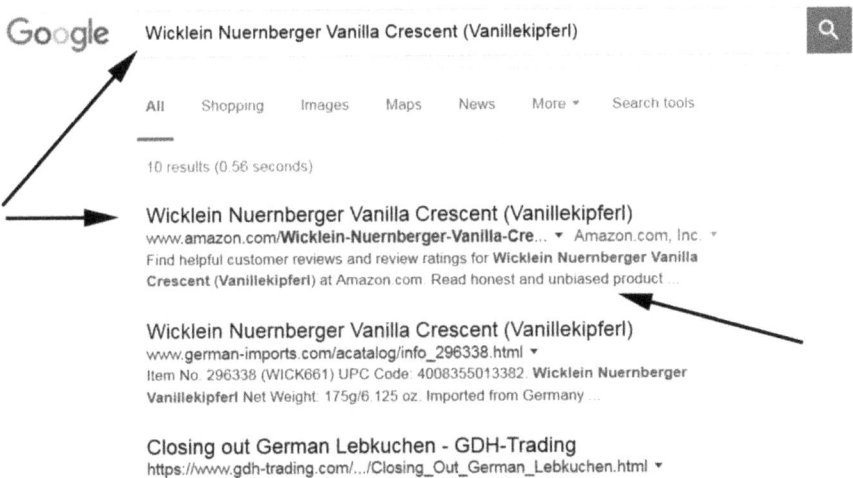

Even today, Americans who have vacationed in Europe, where they may have found out how fabulous Vanillekipferl taste, and who therefore may want to buy them in the U.S., will be led straight to my product review.

What if there were hundreds of reviews? Would my favorite Vanillekipferl still be offered at Amazon.com? I believe so.

Even a completely generic search for "Vanillekipferl review" will show my review in position #10 of the 17,300 search results Google delivers, including recipes and other information potential customers might not want to know – on the first page of the search results.

There is more to the topic of SEO and/or Search Engine Information!

Even if a company optimizes their own website's search engine ranking, Amazon's website will be right there at the top. Amazon's website is about as optimized for search engines as any website can be.

Let's look at an example.

Avon Products, Inc. is the fifth-largest beauty company and second-largest direct-selling enterprise in the world, with 6.4 million representatives, who sell Avon products. Most women know somebody who sells these beauty products. Avon also sells beauty products on Amazon.

When searching for an Avon product, the first search result is (could be) a sponsored posting (marked as AD), which, since it is paid for, is listed in the top position. The next two search results are Avon web pages, and already the third search result is Amazon's page of this particular product.

Notice that the same product enjoys an average rating of 4.4 stars on Avon's site, but only a 4-star rating on Amazon's site. If you were a woman trying to find out more about this particular product, where would you look?

It is for this reason that any business owner or independent contractor, whose products are (also) being sold on Amazon, should aim for getting many great reviews on Amazon. Potential customers are going to check there anyway; so, why not make it easy for them to find best answers?

Additionally, average ratings are a numbers game. The more reviews a product receives, the more accurately it will reflect consumers' reactions. In the company of many good reviews, a few bad ones will lose significance and won't affect the average rating too much.

At some of the small business owners' meetings which I attend, "asking for reviews on Facebook" is a popular topic. Though doing this is certainly a good idea, keep in mind that reviews on Facebook product pages or Facebook store pages will not always show up in Google searches. Also, only the people who already follow a particular product or store will get to see them *if* they care to look, or *if* the business owner pays for Facebook ads. In contrast, Amazon's webpage will always pop up in a top position regardless of where the potential buyer searches.

Since Amazon optimizes their site at no cost to vendors, why not take advantage of this awesome opportunity?

Products need different types of reviews:

Though there is a common perception that all 5-star reviews are great and that all 1-star reviews are bad, this is not true. Only a huge number of 5-star reviews or 1-star reviews may influence customers' general opinions that a product is fabulous or useful; or – not.

If a product has less than 100 reviews almost all customers will scan through these reviews and form their opinions based on what they read. Even if a product has more than 1,000 reviews customers will read many of the reviews.

Don't believe that? To see proof, just check any product with more than 1,000 reviews and see how many reviews have received "likes." Amazon ensures that every potential customer can vote only once, thus the number of "likes" is an indicator of how many people read a review.

Depending on the reviewer and their mood at the time of writing there are different types of reviews. The difference in writing styles appeal to different types of potential customers. Many people appreciate a certain type of review more than others.

For instance, while some people will be pleased to read specifics, such as that a certain item weighs less than 4-1/2 ounces and has such and such dimensions, for other people the word "small" is sufficient to explain the product's size. Some people get even annoyed if they find too many specifics; they would prefer to read overall impressions.

The majority of customers enjoys reading little stories, which they feel apply to their personal situation. For instance a "mini short story" like "I bought this product for my grandmother, who has to use a walker..." paints a complete picture for people who have a relative in the same situation. For this type of customer a technical review may be unattractive. In contrast, for a really tall or a short person, reading a technical review that features specific dimensions can be the deciding factor to buy the product.

Even a 1-or-2-star review may not cause any substantial damage. For instance, if a reviewer awarded a pest repeller, which is supposed to work for all kinds of pests, with only 2-stars because the product did not prove to be effective against mice, a potential buyer, whose home is plagued by roaches and ants could care less. The reviewer's problem is not theirs.

Again other people just want to find out that hundreds and hundreds of people bought a product and awarded it with 5 stars. Once they see confirmation, that is the deciding factor for clicking the "Add to Cart"-button.

Therefore, a good mix of all different types of reviews will help the sales of a product the most.

7 TYPES OF REVIEWS

The "I just want to say 'I love this'" review

Typically, this type of review does not give any technical specifications; it is more or less an acknowledgement that the reviewer liked the product. The more reviews a product acquires, the more likely consumers will post this type of review. If a product already features a lot of reviews, some reviewers feel that everything important about the product has already been said; therefore they keep their own comments short.

Examples of this type of review:

- The best (product) in the world!!!
- BEST
- Great (product)!

A more sophisticated example of this type of review is my evaluation of the previously mentioned Star Wars Adult Jedi Fleece Hooded Bath Robes. My review gives a few specifications, tells about the psychological benefit of this purchase for me, the buyer, and it also features a picture.

★★★★★ **we are Jedis - now!**, January 13, 2016
By Gisela Hausmann
(Edit review) (Delete review)
Verified Purchase (What's this?)
This review is from: **Star Wars Adult Jedi Fleece Hooded Bath Robe (Apparel)**
Bought three for Christmas - two for my kids and one for me.

What can I say... We are Jedis now!
Parents of millennials will know that these days kids have opinions about "parents' parental gifts." Whereas my generation wore awful looking sweaters with disgust when we visited grandma, children no longer do this, even if the gift is a five star rated tech device. Millennials have grown up with the ability to find the "latest" information and they want to buy themselves.

That being said, my Christmas gifts of "Star Wars Jedi Fleece Bathrobes" was more than appreciated. My children wore them all morning and it is a safe bet that they will wear these bathrobes every morning. I am 5'8", my son is 5'11, and my daughter is 6'1." The robe fits me perfectly, it's touching my feet on the top, it reaches my daughter's ankles (which is much longer than any other morning robe she has ever owned), and son's reaches in between feet and ankles.

Love them, love them, love them.

Soft, fluffy, wonderful - we are Jedis - now.

The Typical Customer Review

The typical customer review will state how much the buyer liked or didn't like the product. Every single one should be read by the manufacturer to address customers' needs in the future.

Most typical customer reviews are between three to six lines long. If customers invest even more time by sharing their opinions in an even longer review, most certainly their thoughts should be taken seriously. Every review advances interesting information for fellow shoppers as well as for the manufacturer of the product. Instead of having to hire a consumer research company, the manufacturer and the vendor receive the benefit of a consumer's opinion for free.

The Technical Review

The technical review is characterized by featuring measurements, dimensions, and specifications. Often, the reviewer quotes the product's manual and/or elaborates if the manual is instructive or not. Sometimes, the reviewer includes pictures or videos to demonstrate how the product works, and/or if a particular function doesn't work well.

Not surprisingly, certain items, e.g. electronics or tools receive more reviews of this type but I have also seen many technical reviews of kitchen tools and even food items.

The Venting Review

Sadly, not every customer will be happy; some unhappy customers articulate their opinions in reviews. While most manufacturers/

vendors will be disappointed, it is obvious that not every product will make every consumer happy.

At Amazon.com, even books from Nobel laureates in Literature receive 1-star reviews. Hemingway's *The Old Man and the Sea* received ninety-seven 1-star reviews and John Steinbeck's *The Grapes of Wrath* received sixty-eight 1-star reviews (as of January 2016). Things happen.

The Funny Review

The funny review will do one thing better than all other types of reviews – it gets people talking, at the water cooler! I have even seen funny reviews with pictures. I wish all vendors to be so lucky, that a truly funny man/ woman reviews their product(s). These funny reviews get blogged about and recommended; most certainly any product featured in an exceptional funny review will get exposure.

Quite famous among the funny reviewers is American actor, director, author, and activist George Takei. Personally, I like his review of the "Ninja Folding Grappling Hook" best.

Though he has stopped reviewing, many of George Takei's reviews can be found online.

Funny reviews also attract more reviews. Amazon reviewers know that funny reviews will receive attention for a long time, hence many of them will be interested to review "the lucky product." Also, reviewing an item that is "in the news" is more exciting than reviewing an item few consumers check out.

For instance, George Takei reviewed "The Mountain Three Wolf Moon Short Sleeve Tee. " As of today this T-shirt has received more than 3,000 customer reviews and close to 40 "answered questions." George Takei's review has been found helpful over 10,000 times which goes to show that any product featured in an exceptional funny review will get exposure.

Please see this review at: **https://tinyurl.com/h462vay**

The Short Story Review

Generally speaking, the short story review is most powerful for the majority of people, *if* they can relate to the presented story. Potential customers really want to know only one thing, "Will this product work for me?"

A "short story review" that describes a situation the potential buyer can relate to, and also offers information on how the specific product helped, is most often the most effective tool.

Of all reviews, the short story review is the hardest one to obtain. Consumers either have a story to offer, or not.

The Top Reviewer or Hall of Fame Reviewer's Review

A review posted by an Amazon Top Reviewer or even a Hall of Fame reviewer is a quality mark.

Customers value reviews from Amazon top reviewers a lot. Whereas most people only review products they actually use, Amazon top reviewers also test and review products for the specific purpose of testing or market research. Therefore, they may have experience with many similar products from different manufacturers. Many Amazon top reviewers are also known experts in their respective fields.

Hall of Fame reviewers have huge numbers of followers.

Obviously, it is a problem for vendors that under the changed guidelines they cannot offer sample products to **Amazon top reviewer** or **Hall of Fame** reviewers any longer.

However, in this book, I will propose some other clever concepts that will help.

7 TIPS HOW TO BOOST SALES

1) Learn from reviews

- Value them!
- Learn from them!
- Discuss them with your Product Development department!

Reviews feature customers' opinions. Considering how expensive market research can be, it is beyond me how many producers, manufacturers, and vendors seem to ignore their customers' opinions.

On September 25, 2013, I reviewed the
Algreen 81002 Agua 50-Gallon Rain Water Collection and Storage System (Lawn & Patio) – **4 stars**

***

Title of review:
It's a great looking barrel, but forget the planter, By Gisela Hausmann

"... This rain barrel is probably the most beautiful on the market. Having owned one for over a year I can state honestly that it does not discolor or fade. It looks just as good as when I bought it, even though it is exposed to bright sunlight every day.

In times of decent rainfall, this rain barrel holds enough water for my three veggie beds.

However, it needs to be noted that I had to experiment with how high the barrel needs to be propped up. Right now I have it sitting on two rows of cinder blocks, which is high enough to get the right water pressure for draining.

The reason why I do not give this rain barrel 5 stars is because the cute looking planter is not usable as a planter. It has no drainage, thus if it rains for two days any plants in this planter in the molded barrel will drown. I have replaced the plants with decorative stones and a little garden sculpture, which makes the whole arrangement look even better.

Gisela Hausmann, "green" living author & blogger..."

***

I believe this to be a review that points out the strengths of this particular item and also offers solutions for its tiny problems. This review states

facts about the product

- does not discolor or fade
- the cute looking planter is not usable as a planter because it has no drainage, therefore plants will drown in it
- holds enough water for my three veggie beds

facts about the reviewer's personal usage

- owned the rain barrel for over a year

- it is exposed to bright sun light every day
- barrel is sitting on two rows of cinder blocks, which is high enough to get the right water pressure for draining
- replaced the plants in the planter with decorative stones and a little garden sculpture

personal impressions of the reviewer (free marketing)

- great looking barrel
- probably the most beautiful barrel on the market

***

Why do I believe that this products' manufacturer never read my review or used it for their market research?

I posted my review on September 25, 2013, two years and five months ago. It never received even only one "like" and nobody commented on it.

Looking at the reviews other reviewers had posted, it becomes clear that I noted the same issues some other reviewers observed already in 2008. The manufacturer could have printed a remark,

> "Please note: To encourage the water flow, please elevate this rain barrel by putting it on a steady surface like cinder blocks. Raising the barrel x to y number of inches from the ground will lead to best results..."

on a label, which could have been affixed on the barrel quite easily. The label could even include a technical drawing. I am guessing that a market research firm would have recommended doing that.

If indeed the label would have been improved to include such a comment, sometime in 2009, I would have never experienced the same issue in 2013 – four years later!

Yet, even in 2015, people posted reviews stating the same issues reviewers noted in 2008 and I experienced in 2013.

Considering that this type of (review) market research is free of cost, I am baffled. My review makes it clear that the product is fine and does not have to be redesigned. Designing and printing a new label doesn't cost too much money or effort.

It is not unusual or outrageous to think that manufacturers/ vendors/ marketing people should think and work this way. Many industries go to great lengths to receive customers' feedback; some companies spend months conducting field tests.

Routinely, software companies conduct public beta testing. Many movies and television shows are being test screened before they get released or entered in film festivals. While consumers' reviews cannot replace market research, they are a great starting point.

Additionally, this "review market research" is of course beneficial to any business' competition. I am sure that some of them try to solve their competitors' problems to create a better product themselves. In today's open society, in which everybody has access to millions of tidbits of information, it is an absolute necessity to listen to the consumer.

What to do if your product gets a negative review

Though every manufacturer and vendor hopes for great reviews even the best product can receive a 3-star review because the reviewer thinks that the product is only so-so, nothing special, nothing to write home about, or even worse, a 1-star or 2-star review.

The following short story illustrates how at least one author felt about one of my book reviews, a 4-star review.

After I posted my review, the author sent me an email asking

***

"...Curious why 4 instead of 5 stars..."

and later in the email

"... so I feel cheated with 4 stars, just my honest reaction. But your review was presented with excellent panache, which makes the 4 stars all the more puzzling and even *insulting...*"

[Insulting?]

***

This little story is pitiful. The author completely missed his/her chance to learn. Because the author sent me this unfortunate correspondence, I still remember the book. It was a pretty good book but it was too long. Cutting 25% would have made it a better and more successful book.

It the same for products. Nobody gains anything if they don't accept solicited or unsolicited advice. Sometimes, reviewers/ customers may have really good ideas. Most great inventions have come from realizing that there is always room for improvement.

> "Genius is one percent inspiration, ninety-nine percent perspiration." – Thomas Alva Edison

And, that says it all.

Fighting or manipulating reviews does not pay off. A product either helps people to do what they need to do, or not. Sometimes, even the value of the best products is getting lost on a reviewer or customer because

- the reviewer has no experience with the product group
- the customer did not understand how to use the product correctly
- the product could be improved.

Most of those things can be fixed if the manufacturer/ vendor/ marketing people listen to the people the product is made for. After all, it's about the consumer and not about collecting stars. In this competitive world, the best products will sell the best.

Trolls

Trolls should not be confused with people who write negative reviews to articulate their dissatisfaction with a product.

*

Urban Dictionary
troll
> One who posts a deliberately provocative message to a newsgroup or message board with the intention of causing maximum disruption and argument

*

When Amazon put its algorithm designed to find fake reviews to work, the algorithm deleted many tens of thousands of fake positive reviews as well as fake negative reviews. (More about this in various articles on the Internet.)

Though many authors and vendors thought that ever since Amazon took decisive action, this problem was a thing of the past, over the last few months the topic made headlines, again. In September 2016, Hillary Clinton's and Tim Kaine's book *Stronger Together* received hundreds of troll reviews. Mid-November, 2016, TV-personality Megyn Kelly's book became a target; her book *Settle for More* received more than 100 negative reviews within hours of its release, according to *The Los Angeles Times*. Most recently, Ivanka Trump's merchandise collected all kinds of unfriendly reviews, which weren't really product reviews. Clearly, this issue will never go away, completely.

It is common logic that celebrities become victims of trolling more often than "regular vendors" simply because more people have an opinion about them and their products. I too adhered to that concept until recently two of my books got attacked by what I would call a troll who penned two non-Amazon Verified Purchase reviews for two of my books. A bit of research revealed that this particular "reviewer" also reviewed two dozen other authors' books and posted almost identical sounding non-Amazon Verified Purchase reviews. None of them referred to the any of the books' contents but only noted that these are terrible books which should be burned.

If your product receives a troll review, you, like me, could "report abuse" but there is no guarantee that Amazon will agree to our evaluation of what constitutes a troll review.

So, what's the damage?

Personally, I believe that most people can and will recognize a troll review as what it is. Also, most trolls do not buy the products they intend to *criticize* but post non-Amazon Verified Purchase reviews. As mentioned, in February, 2017, Amazon changed the way they display reviews; non-Amazon Verified Purchase reviews aren't being shown automatically. This means that consumers have to elect to pull them up; even a really nasty troll review may not create too much damage.

Therefore, the biggest problem caused by troll reviews isn't what it says; it is the reduced average star-rating.

In December, 2016, *Forbes* reported *Feedvisor's* research that over 90% of people buying on Amazon wouldn't purchase an item with an average rating of less than three stars. Hence, if your product has only six reviews, three of them being 5-star reviews, and the other three being 1-star reviews, you might have a problem.

Though various ecommerce strategists recommend various methods to deal with this problem, in reality there is only one solution for it: Get more authentic positive reviews!

Why do customers trust reviewers they don't even know?

Before customer reviews became the rave, merchants used to hype their advertisements by listing testimonials from all kinds of people, some of them well-known, others not that much. Though there is nothing wrong with this form of advertisement, it isn't objective because none of us has ever seen any advertisement displaying a negative testimonial.

In contrast, reviews posted on a third-party review platform allow customers to announce the complete range of opinions, hence the more reviews a product has, the more people will trust that they display "the truth" about the product's value, usability, and customer satisfaction.

Personally, I never buy any product which is advertised on Facebook. It takes too much time to weed through the scams. However, a while ago, I fell for a product that had something to do with the Dalai Lama. I am big a big fan of his Holiness and even visited Tibet for this reason.

Though "the product" sported over two dozen glowing endorsements from celebrities it didn't even meet my lowest expectations.

The "complete range of opinions" about this product on Amazon:

66% - 5 star, **3%** - 4 star [positive]

7% - 3 star [neutral]

14% - 2 star, **10%** - 1 star [negative]

These numbers show that, in general, Amazon reviews are more objective than "endorsements."

TIP 2) How to find reviewers who write technical reviews
Maybe – at live events?

Reading the new guidelines, you probably noticed that you absolutely cannot offer any incentives (including sample products) *in exchange* for reviews; BUT, strictly speaking, you could give away a certain number of products and "hope for the best."

Since under the new guidelines, potential reviewers are not allowed to enter in an agreement with you that they will review your product, please don't ask for it.

In other words, if you give away products, you are doing so at your own risk.

Also, you cannot ask your employees or affiliates to write reviews but they can answer questions in the Q/A section if they disclose that they work for the company.

Depending on how you market your product, you may still be able to find reviewers at live events, specifically – reviewers who most likely will be posting technical reviews. Maybe you launch your product at a store event, or you present your product via

- event marketing,
- in-store demo campaigns,
- wholesale-store road shows,
- mobile sampling tours,
- festivals,
- fairs?

For instance, I see great opportunities for manufacturers and vendors of food products. Hosting cooking events will only attract "experts in the field," people who really like to cook, which makes them potential expert reviewers for food products. They might enjoy posting reviews to share their own opinions. Given the fact that they are experts, most likely they will post a technical review and not a half-baked comment like "Great Product."

Similarly, vendors of beauty products, office products, tools, and outdoor equipment have their own events, which might offer the same opportunities.

Please note that if you give away products, you shouldn't go overboard. If Amazon never sold a single unit of your product, yet 300 people suddenly post a review, it won't take Sherlock Holmes to figure out what happened. In its latest revision of the Community Guidelines, Amazon even addressed this issue stating that if a product receives *unusually high numbers of reviews* posted in a *short period of time*, they may restrict the number of non-Amazon Verified Purchase reviews on that product.

TIP 3) How to find reviewers who write funny reviews?
Maybe – through social media postings?

Social media followers love fun postings. Twitter has its own fun section, equally important as the categories 'Today', 'Election 2016', 'NFL', 'News', 'Sports', and 'Entertainment'.

Since it's also a proven fact that social media fans appreciate picture postings, it's up to your marketing team to come up with great ideas.

The 21st century is all about ingenuity and sharing.

TIP 4) How to find reviewers who write "I just want to say 'I love this'" reviews
Maybe – by bragging?

There are over 200 millions products and more than 32 million books for sale at Amazon. Clearly, both vendors and authors have to fight for their market share.

Therefore, it is interesting to know that authors approach the topic of bragging about the ones their books have received completely different than vendors.

In general, when authors run a promotion, they "advertise" or mention how many reviews their book(s) have received. And, why not? In the end, it is the potential customers who decide whether these reviews convince them to buy, or not.

In contrast, I have found very few vendors who "advertise" the number of reviews their product has received. Most remarkable is the Squatty Potty's commercial, which can be watched on Youtube. It not only announces that the product has received more than two-thousand 5-star reviews, it also shows the commercial's "actor," an animated unicorn, looking at his smartphone, where some of the 5-star reviews are displayed. (2:00 min into the commercial)

https://youtu.be/YbYWhdLO43Q

Please note that shooting this commercial must have been quite expensive.

Please also note that Amazon's logo is surely trademarked and cannot be featured without asking Amazon for permission.

But still, there must be a way how you can brag tastefully. People who love to discover new products will listen.

If your product has received many reviews, announce it to the world. If it didn't – Get the reviews!

Announcing,

> "Read what others' say about our (product), see its three-hundred 5-star reviews at Amazon..."

might get your potential customers to look at the reviews at the place where they can also buy with one click!

Please note: Reviews are protected by the copyright like all other written materials. To quote verbatim from a review, you need to get permission from the copyright owner (the author of the review).

TIP 5) How to find reviewers who write typical customer reviews?
Maybe – by printing "reminder"-tags?

People who know me will tell you that I am not a clothes horse. I admire Steve Jobs who with one type of garb achieved the same effect as Kim Kardashian. However, when on occasion I do buy clothes, I am amazed at the number of labels attached to women's clothing.

And, being an Amazon eCommerce expert, I wonder why I never see this type of label:

TIP 6) Update your Customer Service Information and make reading reviews part of your Customer Service agents' job description

To see if my long held suspicion that most companies have not "optimized" their process of seeking reviews is true I spent six hours at a shopping supercenter and looked at more than one thousand boxes, packages, and wrappers of every type of product under the sun.

Some of the labels featured concepts that are clearly outdated.

- "Questions or Comments? Write: Consumer Affairs, PO Box, (address)"

I am not sure that the millennials even know how to *write* Consumer Affairs.

Also the remark

- "For questions and comments please call 1-800-xxx-xxxx. Please have code and date information from container."

has issues. Three decades ago, every single product featured this comment. And, customers called; they called often. Then, everybody called about everything. After a decade of consumers complaining about that customer service agents jobs got outsourced overseas, the Internet arrived, and more customer service agents got laid off. Today, this topic can be summed up:

If a company does not offer excellent "live" customer service they need to consider that somebody is going to tell what happened when they called, how long it took till they got a human voice, and everything else that went wrong — in a 1-star or a 2-star review on Amazon. Even if the company changes their ways, that review will never go away.

To test various customer services I called random two dozen companies. The very best customer service agent picked up the phone in only 16 seconds; plus, the lady was charming. I was excited because, indeed, I really buy and use this company's products. [*I might want to review one in the near future.*]

The worst "customer service," if one can even call it that, kept me on the phone with prerecorded messages about their products, for 5 minutes. The 5-minute message included information/ disclaimers that the company wanted to "collect my data" for ... whatever ...

It sounded as if I was listening to Big Brother himself. So, after 5 minutes of this I hung up.

In part, doing this research was even funny.

One of the two dozen companies I called featured a recorded message that announced,

> "To speak to a customer service representative please dial 1. *Rotary phone users* should remain on the line..."

The humor of this statement might be lost for many. 27.3% of the U.S. population is under 20 years of age. They don't know how to make phone calls from a rotary phone. They literally don't understand why the message announces anything about rotary phones.

Why is the quality of a customer service relevant with regards to reviews?

Though the average consumer might not call to share their opinion about a certain product, annoyed or even irate consumers will call. If, when they call, they get a silly "Big Brother"-recording they may not wait to listen but post a review right away.

Customer Review

★★★★★ **Fabulous item + great customer service**, November 26, 2013

By Gisela Hausmann

(Edit review) (Delete review)

Verified Purchase (What's this?)

This review is from: **SmartCat Bootsie's Bunk Bed and Playroom for Cats (Misc.)**

Original review updated to 5*****

Originally, when I bought this cat bunk bed in 2012 I had issues with it; issues, which the manufacturer resolved quickly and to my total satisfaction (Pls see below the update from 12/12/12 to my original review, which I have removed).

Since I now own this item for 2 1/2 years I can say with certainty it is an excellent buy. The item has lasted that long, and it has given my cat continuous pleasure. When she was little she used to play in "the playroom", now that she is more mature, she loves to sleep on the bed. I have two cats, and only the cat for who I bought this bed/toy sleeps and plays in and on it, so it's her territory, probably because she likes it so much.

The toys mounted on the side are still in place, which speaks for the sturdiness and excellent attachment. Especially the fluffy thing (imitation bird) got pulled over and over through the various holes, plus, it also got slapped around quite a bit.

The cushion has collected a bit of cat hair in the seams, even though I remove the cat hair with brush at least once per week. But that's normal. Cat and cat hair go together. I hope the manufacturer will come out with replacement cushions. To be honest I never thought this cat bunk bed would last that long, so I AM pleasantly surprised.

[old update from 12/12/12 to the original 3 star review which since removed. I fully support 5 stars for this product and would recommend it to my best friends]

While the brackets of this particular item may not have been suitable for "rough transport" the customer service of the manufacturing company deserves 5*****. As mentioned, I called them to complain and ask for replacement brackets. The lady, who took the call was particularly friendly, apologized for the brackets being broken in transport, and sent replacement brackets a.s.a.p. Installing the new brackets can be done with a small screw driver of the type used to tighten the screws on glasses. I imagine any small screw driver will do. I will update this review further once my kitty has had enough opportunity to play with the item. Thank you customer service for taking care of this issue in such a speedy way.

Gisela Hausmann, author & blogger
+ kitty Artemis

Only once I had to call customer service regarding a product that arrived with a few parts already broken during transport. The excellent agent did her job so well that I later updated my review.

It is not a rare event. Anybody, who takes the time to scan through product reviews will find many reviews, whose writers share their experiences with "live customer service."

The "live experience" will find its way online, where, when posted in an Amazon customer review, it will do much good or much damage, depending on how good, bad, or even superior the customer service is.

But, don't only focus on "live" communication. Make reading Amazon's Q/A section of all your products a part of your customers service agents' job description. Customers may have questions, which other Amazon shoppers cannot or won't answer correctly. Please remember, that employees have to identify themselves properly.

http://www.amazon.com/gp/community-help/customer-reviews-guidelines

TIP 7) How to find all kinds of reviewers – The best tip of all

Today, we email, we text, we send information via cloud storage services, we barely ever talk on the phone. Our ways of communication have become so sophisticated that often we forget the easiest way of communicating is – the written word.

Additionally, to the previously mentioned remarks, the more than one thousand boxes, packages, and wrappers of every type of product under the sun, listed information like

- 100% Recycled Paperboard
- Gluten Free
- Non GMO
- Visit www...com for complete care instruction and tips...
- Join the conversation with (company) (Facebook logo) (Twitter logo)
- Please recycle
- Made in USA

and dozens of other valuable bits of information.

NOT A SINGLE ONE of them listed, "Please review (this product) on... "

There are literally thousands of items whose boxes have "empty" space. Small appliance boxes, motor oil bottles, cooler boxes, diaper boxes, cereal boxes, laptop and printer boxes, shoe boxes, plastic wrappers of multi-product packages, huge toy boxes, etc. all have empty space with enough room to print "Please review (this product) on... "

It is the 21st century approach.

Most containers offer enough room to add:

"Please share your opinion and review this product on... "

Of course, things don't end there. Your boxes will be transported in trucks that could be considered billboards.

Lots of cars will follow your truck. Therefore consider using this space.

Attention: Please check your state's regulatory requirements before designing the signage.

How to encourage customers to review?

Remind – remind – remind customers that their opinion is valued.

Every product is different, hence you may not have the opportunity to remind customers many times, but maybe it would be fitting to print reminders on various layers of packaging.

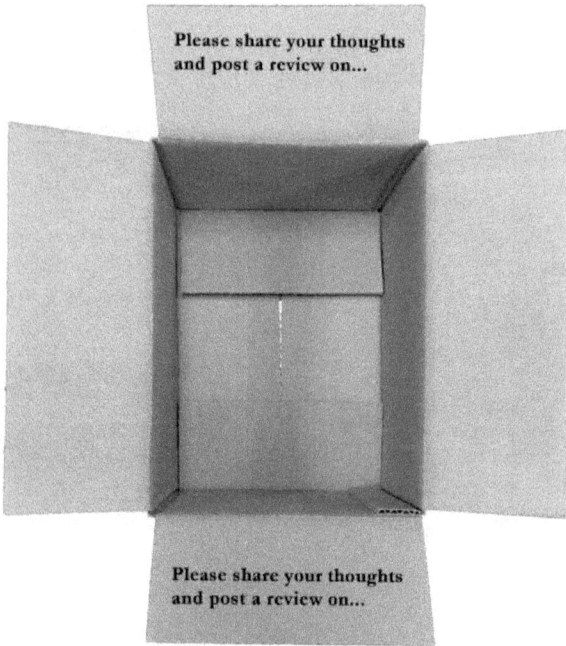

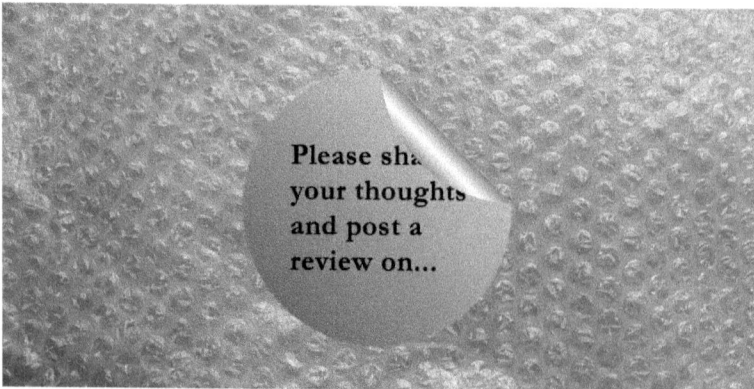

Invite consumers to share a personal story:

Previously, I mentioned that customers either have a story to share in a review, or – not.

Another fact is that customers don't necessarily think about sharing their personal story but you can encourage them. The story could even be shared with a visual. Review readers appreciate reviews with pictures.

A few examples of what you can do:

Attach a label that asks

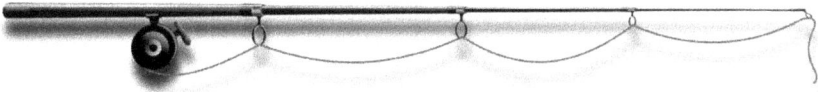

"Please review this fishing rod on ... and also share a picture of the biggest fish you caught"

"What's your running routine? Please share your stats in your review on..."

"Meat or fish? – Please share what you like to grill in your review on..."

"Who is the artist in your family? Please share a picture when reviewing these crayons on ..."

"How cute did baby look? Please post a review and maybe even share a picture on ..."

"Did dad like the tie? Please let us know in a review on ..."

Finally – Where should you start?

As you arrive at the end of this book, you may have already checked how many reviews your product(s) feature. Many questions may be going through your mind like

- Why doesn't my product have more reviews?
- Why do my competitor's products have thousands of reviews?
- Whose job is it to look into this?
- Whose job is it to read and evaluate the reviews our product have received?
- When should I schedule a meeting with the product development department?

and related questions.

The task list could look daunting. Still, you should get to work right away. Always keep in mind, lots of people tried to cheat to get these valuable reviews. Of course, they only tried to cheat because an abundance of reviews will help the sales of their product(s).

Also, Amazon invests quite a bit in keeping the process working as perfect as they can. As with all Internet things time is working against you. If you had bought the original edition of this book when it was released chances are you'd have accumulated a good dozen of reviews from Amazon top reviewers and maybe even from Amazon Hall-of-Fame reviewers. Time is precious now as it was then.

You never know what options you will have in the future thus it will pay off to be proactive now.

TO-DO LISTS

Facts:

Reviews represent customers' opinions!

In our ever-connected world, customers' opinions may be more important than critics' opinions. Whereas a review of a U.S. product in an U.S. magazine may never get read in France or the Netherlands, reviews on Amazon can and are being read around the world.

Work on a strategic plan:

- Compare the reviews your products have received with the reviews your competitors' products have received and see how much work needs to be done. [*Of course, your goal doesn't need to be to garner more reviews than all your competitors collected, but if your products have a combined 100 reviews and your competitors' products have anywhere between 1,000 to 5,000 reviews, it might be time to do something about this.*]
- Check what potential consumers will see if they google your product
- Discuss with your marketing department if and how you can use existing reviews to "brag" in a tasteful way
- Create a marketing plan on how you can integrate product reviews in your existing marketing plan (commercials, ads, presentations etc.)

Evaluate the reviews:

- Have reviewers mentioned issues your company's Product Development department has not addressed?
- Did your products receive different types of reviews (technical reviews, short-story reviews, typical customer reviews)?
- Have you scanned your competitors' products' reviews for creative and useful ideas?

Evaluate your company's strategic plan to "attract" reviews:

- Does your company have a plan?
- How quickly can you print a request for reviews on your product boxes and other spaces?

Summing it up, here is how savvy manufacturers/ vendors/ marketing people maneuver through the Amazon jungle.

Use the sum of information and benefits to launch new products

Find ways to engage your customers

Acknowledge and evaluate your customers' input

Develop a strategic plan how to get reviews for your product(s)

Check what potential customers will see if they google your product

Compare the number of reviews your products received with the number of reviews your competitors' products garnered

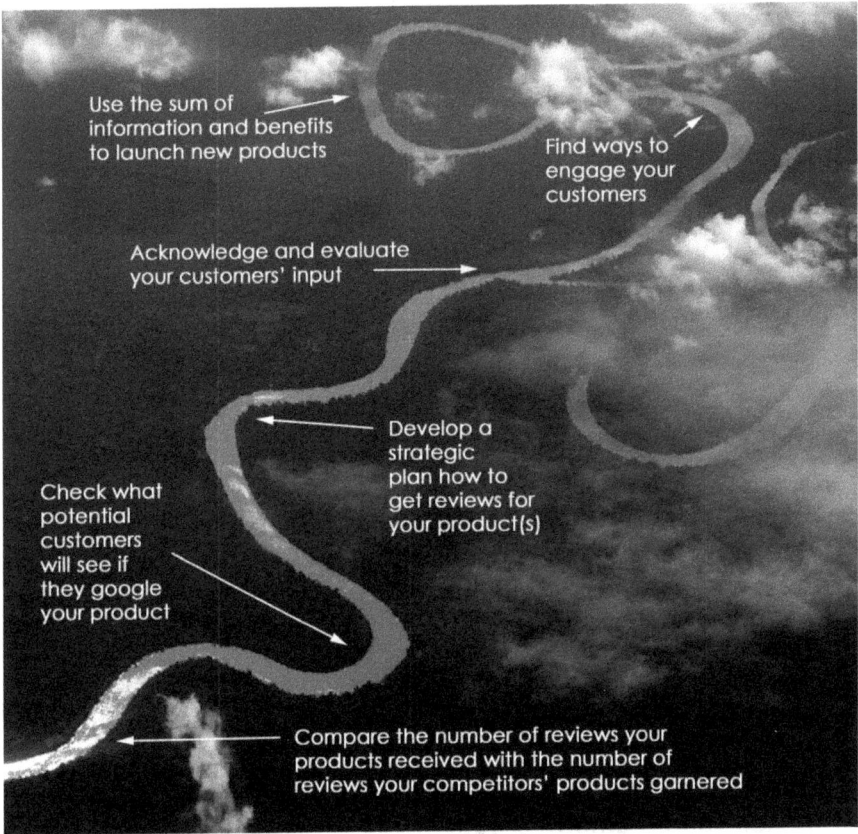

Thank you for reading my book.

- Please contact me with your **success stories**. Maybe I can present them in a future book.

- Please **recommend this book to your business friends** who sell online

- Please **review** this book on Amazon.com. I truly appreciate your opinion, and I am looking for your valued input. Thank you!

http://www.amazon.com/Gisela-Hausmann/e/B000APN192

Gisela Hausmann's business philosophy about "naked (meaning no-fluff) books"

While I don't know how you learned about my book, my work is not just this book, it is of a whole series of books featuring only "naked (no-fluff) information." Today, thousands of books get published every day; many of them feature a lot of fluff. I know that you don't have time to "work" your way through this fluff, because neither do I.

This is my books' concept:

1) "Naked" how-to books deliver knowledge in the **shortest, most efficient and most entertaining** manner; they are supported by illustrations, which show and tell.

2) "Naked" no-fluff books energize readers, because they do not have to labor through the pages, but can **see what works and why** it works.

3) "Naked" books **empower readers** because reading no-fluff books builds up energy. Readers do not feel drained but feel energized from learning dozens of easy-to-follow strategies and solutions in a short time.

4) "Naked" is to books what **"lean"** is to business; waste information is removed, solutions and action steps are introduced.

5) **"Naked" no-fluff books are so 21st century**... Today, we do not have time to dig for solutions, we want to buy, learn, and win!

Please find more of my books at:

http://www.giselahausmann.com/books.html

To get informed when I release a new "naked (no-fluff) book" please subscribe here. As an email evangelist I do not inundate people with a constant stream of email; it does not work.

Every three months I send a list of my newly published blogs just in case you missed one.

http://www.giselahausmann.com

About the Author

Gisela Hausmann is a marketing and mass media expert.

She is also an email evangelist.

The author of eighteen books, she publishes books under her "naked" brand of books, meaning Gisela publishes "no-fluff" books.

Born to be an adventurer, Gisela has also co-piloted single-engine planes, produced movies, and worked in the industries of education, construction, and international transportation. Gisela's friends and fans know her as a woman who goes out to seek the unusual and rare adventure.

A unique mixture out of wild risk-taker and careful planner, Gisela globe-trotted almost 100,000 kilometers on three continents, including to the locations of her favorite books: Doctor Zhivago's Russia, Heinrich Harrer's Tibet, and Genghis Khan's Mongolia.

Gisela Hausmann graduated with a master's degree in Film & Mass Media from the University of Vienna. She now lives in Greenville, South Carolina.

She tweets at https://twitter.com/Naked_Determina

***

Subscribe to occasional updates at
http://www.giselahausmann.com

More books:

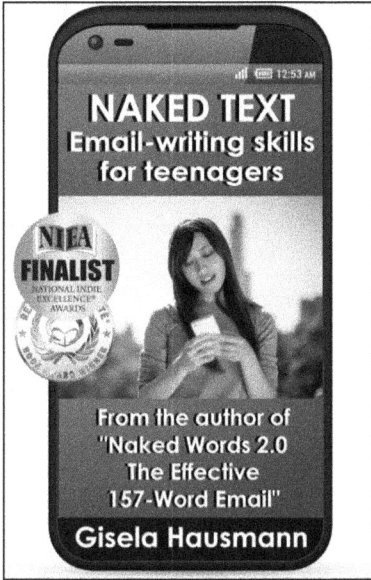

NAKED TEXT
Email-writing skills for teenagers

NIEA FINALIST
NATIONAL INDIE EXCELLENCE® AWARDS

From the author of "Naked Words 2.0 The Effective 157-Word Email"

Gisela Hausmann

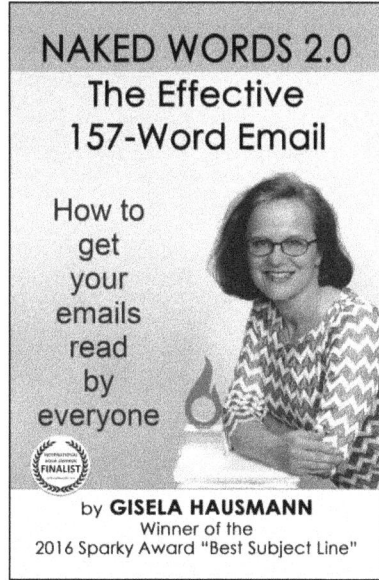

NAKED WORDS 2.0
The Effective 157-Word Email

How to get your emails read by everyone

FINALIST

by GISELA HAUSMANN
Winner of the
2016 Sparky Award "Best Subject Line"

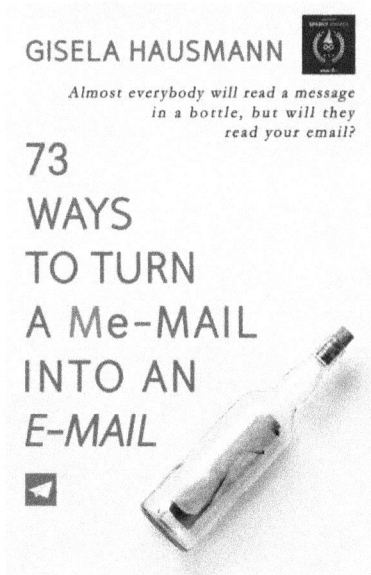

GISELA HAUSMANN

Almost everybody will read a message in a bottle, but will they read your email?

73 WAYS TO TURN A Me-MAIL INTO AN E-MAIL

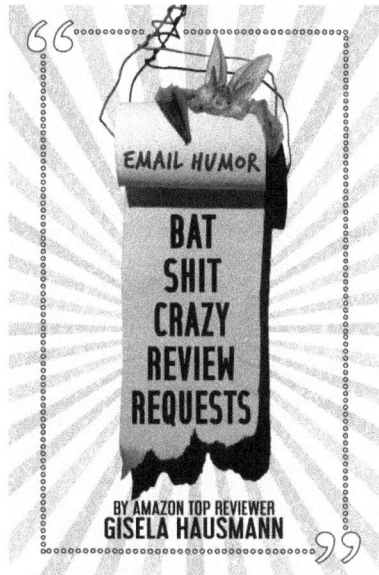

EMAIL HUMOR

BAT SHIT CRAZY REVIEW REQUESTS

BY AMAZON TOP REVIEWER
GISELA HAUSMANN

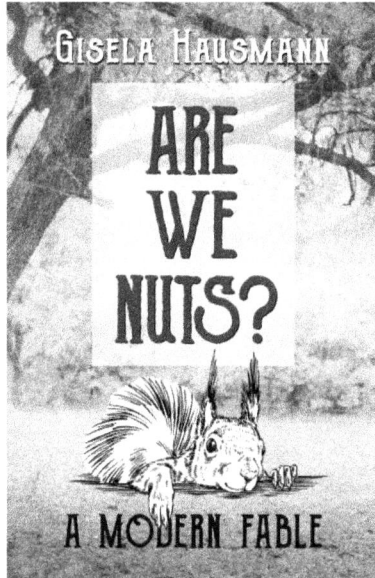

GISELA HAUSMANN

ARE
WE
NUTS?

A MODERN FABLE

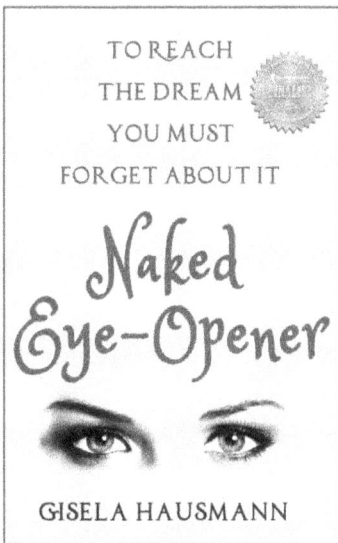

TO REACH
THE DREAM
YOU MUST
FORGET ABOUT IT

Naked
Eye-Opener

GISELA HAUSMANN

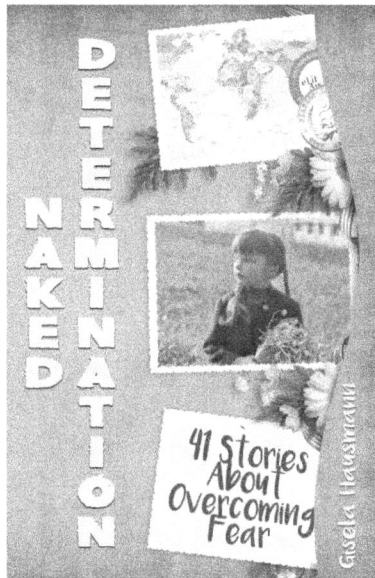

NAKED DETERMINATION

41 Stories
About
Overcoming
Fear

Gisela Hausmann